Fresh Air...

50 Ways to Experience the Best Things About Country Life... Wherever You Live!

Julie Murphree

Trafford Publishing

Fresh Air... 50 Ways to Experience the Best Things About Country Life... Wherever You Live!

Note for Librarians: A cataloguing record for this book is available from Library and Archives Canada at www.collectionscanada.ca/amicus/index-e.html
ISBN 1-4120-9106-3

Acknowledgements:

Jennifer Jones, cover photo

Heather Durham, art director

Sarah Murray, editorial consultant

Photo restoration on certain inside photos by Photo Fix Pro

Printed on paper with minimum 30% recycled fibre.
Trafford's print shop runs on "green energy" from solar, wind and other environmentally-friendly power sources.

PUBLISHING™
Offices in Canada, USA, Ireland and UK

Book sales for North America and international:
Trafford Publishing, 6E–2333 Government St.,
Victoria, BC V8T 4P4 CANADA
phone 250 383 6864 (toll-free 1 888 232 4444)
fax 250 383 6804; email to orders@trafford.com
Book sales in Europe:
Trafford Publishing (UK) Limited, 9 Park End Street, 2nd Floor
Oxford, UK OX1 1HH UNITED KINGDOM
phone 44 (0)1865 722 113 (local rate 0845 230 9601)
facsimile 44 (0)1865 722 868; info.uk@trafford.com
Order online at:
trafford.com/06-0862

10 9 8 7 6 5 4 3 2 1

To all my family and friends – and especially my Maricopa Family –
thank you for enriching my life.

I also dedicate this book to every person who clothes and feeds us daily;
the American farmer.

Contents

Introduction 13

Plant sunflowers 16

Plant pumpkins 17

Go to a pumpkin patch in the fall 18

Plant an herb garden 19

Dry your herbs 22

Plant a community garden 23

Say "Hi." 26

Bake an apple pie (Or your specialty dish) and take to a neighbor 27

Participate in a modern-day barn raising 30

Obtain a copy of Barbara Mandrell & George Jones
version of "I Was Country When Country Wasn't Cool"
(written by Kye Fleming & Dennis Morgan,
charted Country #No. 1 in 1981) 32

Stargaze 34

Obtain CDs with the sounds of nature 38

Decorate a room in country or cowboy motif 39

Invest in a few country decorating books 42

Subscribe to a country living or rural life magazine 44

Blow up and frame old photos of country or rural life 45

Use country scents around your home 46

Join 4-H as a leader 47

Become a financial supporter of F.F.A 49

Travel to a farm 50

Read the Little House series by Laura Ingalls Wilder 51

Read Rebecca of Sunnybrook Farm 54

Read Zane Grey Novels 56

Ride a horse 57

Buy a cowboy hat, then head to the rodeo .59

Go to a western store 60

Attend a tractor pull 62

Go to the county fair 63

Go to the state fair 64

Make the most of harvest time 65

Learn to square dance, country swing or line dance 68

Shop at a farmers' market 69

Watch old westerns 72

Find out what crops grow in your state 73

Adopt a farm family 76

Attend and/or participate in a cow-pie throwing contest 77

Wear cotton 79

Do denim 80

Cook an old-fashioned country meal 81

Plant a tree 82

Explore your family history 83

Plan your vacation to take your family history one step further 85

Help a teacher with Ag in his/her classroom 87

Pick your favorite farm animal and learn about it 89

Visit your local Ag Extension Service 91

Study agriculture in America 92

Work on a farm or ranch 94

Host a party near a country-style landmark .96

Visit a dude ranch 97

Attend church 99

Epilogue 105

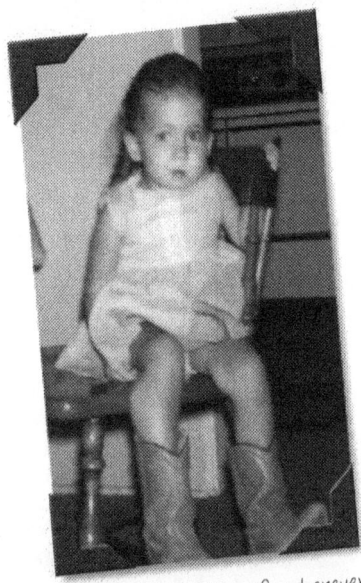

Introduction

Experience country life wherever
by wearing your cowboy boots
everywhere and the country girl
will stay with you.
Author, Julie Murphree

Do you miss country life? Or, having never lived in the country but having romanticized it, do you simply wish you were part of the lifestyle? We close our eyes and imagine fresh air, long walks down an abandoned country road, and expansive vistas. No worries, no packing, no uprooting needed. Just read this "how-to" book to discover ways to live the best parts of the country or rural life minus the flies and manure. You can even stick to the romanticizing!

This book's list of 50 tips provides simple, delightful ways to capture a slice of country or rural life, and you'll never have to step on a fresh cow pie. It doesn't matter where you live! If you apply just a few of the 50 tips, the "ways of the country" become educational for you and your children and you'll feel a part of America's rural heritage. Why not apply splashes of country to your day-to-day to get the best from an idyllic, yet rarified existence but still have easy access to the conveniences of modern-day life in the city and suburbs.

How do I know these tips work? I grew up on a cotton farm in southern Arizona near a small (but growing) town called Maricopa and presently live in the Phoenix suburbs. My Dad, Pat, and Mom, Pennee, along with my three brothers Brent, Patrick and Curt were central to our rural adventures. Every one of my fondest childhood memories sends me back down the dirt road that led to that comforting home nestled between cotton and alfalfa fields. When I want to walk down memory lane or resurrect some part of my special growing-up years I simply play country music, work in my back yard, or watch an old western on television. So, it's true in my case that you can take the girl out of the country, but with a little creativity you can keep the country in the girl.

And country I am. Though I've lived in the "burbs" for nearly 18 years, most of my social activities, volunteer involvement, and outdoor activities plop me in the midst of agriculture- and rural-related settings even today. One of my favorite social activities to look forward to each year is the Casa Grande Valley Cotton and Agriculture Women's annual harvest party in late September. At the harvest party, you can wear your Rockies (western wear jeans for women) and boots, kick up your heels, and pop the top on an ice cold beer.

Friends and family have always been intensely curious about farm and rural life. And even as fewer of us farm for a living, Future Farmers of America (now the National FFA Organization; see Tip No. 19) membership has reached new highs. Farmers' markets (Tip No. 32) across the country continue to gain popularity, and more families plan vacations away from the big city. The more urban and suburban we become, the more farm life seems to fascinate us.

Of course, country folk might chuckle that we romanticize the agrarian life, since staying up all night to irrigate cotton fields, for example, contains not an ounce of romantic bliss. But wait, my friends that still farm tell me pulling an all-nighter does have its benefits: peace and quiet out in the middle of nowhere.

Part of the allure is rural America's onlys. Only in the country will you hear the rhythmic croaking of frogs at night. Only in the country, separated from city lights, will you feel so close to the stars in the night sky that it looks like you could reach out to pluck them one by one and attempt to stuff them in your Levi pocket. Only in the country can you lie out under the same night sky and draw in the sweet smell of fresh-cut alfalfa. Only in the country can you still ride up to your neighbor's house on a horse. We draw upon rural America's limitless storehouse of beauty, lore, and infinite truths to inspire us.

Though many of the tips in this book require boning up on the "how to," simply "Google" or "Yahoo" them on the Internet or go to your nearest Agriculture Extension Service agency, for example, to learn how to plant a sunflower or start an herb garden. Finally, the 50 tips are designed around your five senses — touch, taste, smell, hear, and see — to capture the full grace of country living. So let's begin the adventure.

The List

1

Plant sunflowers.

When Mom planted an early spring garden she'd always seed a row of sunflowers at the end of the garden bed, forming a background. A row of sunflowers brings color variation to a garden and reminds me of miniature slices of sunshine.

Native to North America, the genus Helianthus was used by early North American Indians for food and pressed to make hair oil. Meal from the processed sunflower seed has also been used for livestock feed. Today, whole seeds are used for oil, bird seed and snacks. Sunflower seeds are a rich source of calcium plus a number of other minerals.

So how do you satisfy the gardener in you? Because the sunflower is a rapid grower that reaches heights of 8 to 12 feet in rich soil with adequate water-holding capacity, plant seeds into moistened soil ½ to 1-inch deep. Space seeds 12 inches apart in rows spaced 2- to 2 ½-feet apart. Expert gardeners tell us to space them even further apart for very large plant heads. Begin planting when soil temperatures are around 50 degrees Fahrenheit. With little seedlings popping up in seven to 12 days, plants will mature in 80 to 90 days. When the fully-developed flower goes to seed, you can salt and dry the sunflower seeds for a snack.

Plant pumpkins.

As a way to prepare yourself for the fall season, start your own pumpkin patch. This warm-season vegetable is fairly easy to grow. Mom would sometimes add a few pumpkin seeds to the garden later in the growing season just so we'd have pumpkins in the fall. Although our Halloween pumpkins, once they matured, usually ended up covered in gnats or turned into makeshift kick balls that would burst on contact, we knew that once they had turned a solid orange autumn was on the way.

Because pumpkin seeds do not germinate in cold soil and seedlings are injured by frost, plant pumpkins for Halloween from late May in Northern locations to early July in extremely Southern areas. If pumpkins are planted too early, they may soften and rot before Halloween. Vining pumpkins require a minimum of 50- to 100-square-feet per hill. Plant seeds 1-inch deep (four or five seeds per hill) and allow 5 to 6 feet between each hill, spaced in rows 10 to 15 feet apart. When the young plants are well-established, thin each hill, leaving the best two to three plants. Miniature and bush varieties require different spacing. Check planting instructions on seed packets or look up "planting pumpkins" on the Web to obtain more information.

Pumpkins can be harvested whenever they are a deep, solid color (orange for most varieties) and the rind is hard. If vines remain healthy, harvest in late September or early October before heavy frosts. If the vines die prematurely from disease or other causes, harvest the mature fruit and store them in a moderately warm, dry place until Halloween. Cut pumpkins from the vines carefully, using pruning shears or a sharp knife, and leave 3 to 4 inches of stem attached. Avoid snapping the stems from the vines, as you'll end up with broken or missing vine "handles;" for some reason, pumpkins without stems usually do not keep well. And don't forget to wear your gardener's gloves when harvesting, since several varieties have sharp prickly stems.

3

Go to a pumpkin patch in the fall.

Okay, so planting and growing pumpkins might be a bit daunting, but how about visiting a pumpkin patch during the fall? Loading up the family SUV and heading to outlying areas where large pumpkin patches are located has become a tradition with many families, especially when their children are little. What better setting to photograph the children, surrounded by the large pumpkins stacked around them? One of my favorite autumn photos is of my friend's little boy popping his head up amongst a heap of bright orange pumpkins.

While you can always find the right pumpkin in the nearest supermarket, the adventure of selecting your own from a field holds more magic and adventure. Children obtain a hands-on experience of where their food comes from and parents enjoy the memories they create from the visit to the pumpkin patch. Remember to take your camera!

4

Plant an herb garden.

Though my very first herb garden only produced parsley, despite the fact that I planted several different types of herbs, an herb garden is actually quite simple to start and grow. For example, if you love Italian food and like to cook it with fresh ingredients, you probably already grow basil. The same logic works with country cooking and special herbs. During the summer, I loved it when Mom would send us out to pick mint for our iced tea that she served during lunch.

As the urbanite, if you have to grow your herbs inside select a South or West window. Different herbs have different light requirements, but most need a sunny location; in winter, "grow lamps" or fluorescent lamps are wonderfully helpful in supplementing light. When planting, mix two parts sterilized potting soil and one part coarse sand or perlite. To ensure sweetness of the soil, add a cut of ground limestone per bushel of soil or 1 teaspoon of lime per 5-inch pot. Try an inch of gravel at the bottom of each pot to ensure good drainage.

Most herb packages will state the water needs of each herb. Growing plants need more water than do plants in clay pots or hanging baskets. Misting and grouping the plants on a tray of moistened pebbles will help keep them in humid conditions. Don't drench herbs; soggy herb roots create unhealthy plants.

Annual herbs can spend their full life cycle in a pot indoors. Perennial herbs, however, will do better if you place them outdoors during the summer. Plunge the pots in soil up to their rims, or keep the pots in a protected location on the porch or patio.

Your herb plants love the sun during summer months, but to prevent foliage loss and to avoid plant damage, bring herbs indoors before the first frost comes. However, for mint, chives, and tarragon do allow a light frost; it apparently induces a rest period and makes the resulting new growth firm and fresh.

The indoor herb garden experts maintain their little green oasis indefinitely by periodic light feeding, yearly repotting, renewing annuals, seasonal moves outdoors for perennials, and occasional pruning.

An Internet search or books in the library or bookstore can set you up for life as you create your one-of-a-kind herb garden.

My later attempts with herbs did improve, but I still grow parsley the best. ✤

MY PERSONAL LIST

My Favorite Herbs to Grow
(Check 'My Favorite Recipes' list
for ideas on herbs to grow)

☐ _____

☐ _____

☐ _____

☐ _____

☐ _____

☐ _____

☐ _____

☐ _____

☐ _____

☐ _____

☐ _____

☐ _____

☐ _____

☐ _____

5
Dry your herbs.

Dried herbs smell wonderful, make you feel as though you're in harvest time and bring back all sorts of memories of the country life. Yes, you can find dry herbs just about anywhere but why not make your own? Farm families of recent decades (for example, the Andersons of Maricopa) have experimented with herbs, flowers and other plant varieties suitable for growing and drying and are now part of their diversified farm operations.

If you decide to grow an herb garden, you'll find that home-dried herbs can be just as wonderful as the store-bought variety. In fact, the best dried herbs come from the tender, flavorful leaves from the upper 6 inches of stalk. Leafy stems can be dried in bunches and hung in a well-ventilated, dust-free room to dry. When tying in bunches, use a rubber band. As the plants dry and the stems get smaller, the bunch will not fall apart.

Most herbs are at their peak flavor just before flowering, so this is a good time to collect them for drying and storage. You can even use microwave ovens to dry small quantities of herbs. The moisture content of herbs is extremely low, so place them on a small container of water in the oven [or microwave] during drying. To be certain about the process, check drying directions on specific herbs in a reliable reference book. ✑

Plant a community garden.

Community-grown gardens were popular as far back as the 1940s especially during World War II when communities came together as a result of the war to grow Victory Gardens. The concept even has an association — the American Community Gardening Association. Over the years interest in coordinating a community or urban garden has been driven by a desire to use gardens as a training ground for urban development. These types of gardens include training at-risk youth and adults about horticultural and landscaping, marketing to exclusive restaurants or farmers' markets, and making byproducts such as vinegars and jellies. Though our family never participated in a community garden, the gardens we grew became a source of our giving amongst family and friends. Growing a community garden teaches the principal of reaping. I learned from my own hands digging in the dirt preparing our garden that we must sow seed before we can reap a harvest, and with nurture and care we'll always reap more than we sow. As a result, we always grew enough produce to give away after we filled our own storehouse.

Today's restaurant market sees the bottom line value in gardens. Signature restaurants (especially in New York and Chicago) feature their own specialty vegetables that go straight from the garden to plate — after a thorough washing of course.

Often, however, the idea behind a community garden either in the suburb or city is simply to create a worthwhile community activity that allows neighbors to come together and do something worthwhile. Children love learning how to grow plants and vegetables. Plus, harvest time for the neighborhood community garden can become a big event. To learn how to organize and start your own, link to the American Community Gardening Association Web site at www.communitygarden.org.

MY PERSONAL LIST

My Spring Garden Plans
(What vegetables do I want to grow?)

☐ _____

☐ _____

☐ _____

☐ _____

☐ _____

☐ _____

☐ _____

☐ _____

☐ _____

☐ _____

☐ _____

☐ _____

☐ _____

☐ _____

7

Say 'Hi.'

Wave and visit with your neighbors. We didn't pass a truck on the dirt road leading away from our home in Maricopa, Arizona, without waving at the passengers inside. Then, when we went into town we could never be on time to appointments as everyone was stopping one another on the street to get the latest update on family news.

You live in the city? Make your smile and hello count with those living on your block. When time permits, stop your neighbor and ask them to tell you their latest story, or simply, "What's up?" Even if they balk at first they'll get used to your neighborly friendliness; it becomes a natural part of who you are. Walking the dog opens doors for you to be neighborly. Who hasn't used the line, "Oh, your dog is so cute!" Babies in strollers generate our easiest conversations.

Many block watch programs are centered on the idea of getting to know your neighbor in order to determine what's "out of the norm," and problems can be rectified quickly before true trouble occurs.

It's really not hard to be neighborly, it's just time-consuming. So what in your day can you give up to spend some brief moments being neighborly?

8

Bake an apple pie (or your specialty dish), and take it to a neighbor.

Everyone loved Grandma's Apple pie. So, she made a tradition of baking one for new neighbors in her community. Or, someone just recovering from illness got one. She even made her own pie crusts with extra ones on hand in order to be ready for the next neighbor she wanted to bless. Continuing the neighborly theme, what's one of your favorite dishes that everybody loves? Pick the one dish that gets the most compliments. It's a shoo-in with a new neighbor if the dish gets high marks from others.

GRANDMA'S APPLE PIE

6-8 Granny Smith or Pippin apples

½ cup brown sugar

⅛ teaspoon cloves

½ cup raisins (optional)

4 teaspoons flour

1 ½ ounce rum. (It was the rum.)

1 10 inch, 2 crust pie shell

½ cup granulated sugar

1 teaspoon cinnamon

⅛ teaspoon nutmeg

½ cup pecans, chopped

⅛ cup butter

1 fresh lemon

Peel, core and slice apples. Squeeze fresh lemon over apples. Mix all other ingredients. Bring to a boil. Pour over apples and mix well.

For the crust:

Blend flour, salt and shortening until mixture is crumbly. Add water; form into smooth ball and divide in half. Roll out each half separately; line 10-inch pie pan with pastry. Pour apple mixture into pastry-lined pan; top with pastry shell. Combine egg and cream in small bowl; brush on top of pastry. Bake at 425 degrees for 15 minutes. Reduce heat to 350 degrees for 40-45 minutes. Yield: One 10-inch pie.

Pie Option 2: Just go get a pie from a local bakery. I know I would not turn one down if a neighbor came by my house with one!

MY PERSONAL LIST

My Best Recipes

- [ ] _____
- [ ] _____
- [ ] _____
- [ ] _____
- [ ] _____
- [ ] _____
- [ ] _____
- [ ] _____
- [ ] _____
- [ ] _____
- [ ] _____
- [ ] _____
- [ ] _____
- [ ] _____
- [ ] _____

9

Participate in a modern-day barn raising.

Though you or a neighbor might not need a barn built, a modern-day barn raising activity could be as simple as helping a neighbor trying to install his own sprinkler system or finishing a landscape project. And what about the neighbor trying to put in pathway lighting? If you've just completed the project yourself, you'd be the perfect one to help him.

One recent and unique example of the modern-day barn raising involves some friends of my parents, the Echeverrias, who built their house out of oversized straw bales for insulation and environmental reasons. To create the walls, neighbors from everywhere showed up for a day-long project that resulted in a nearly completed house although not a single nail was hammered.

Straw bale construction is an old building method that has undergone a revival in recent years, especially in the American Southwest. Straw bales were first used in construction in Nebraska in the late 1800s. Some of these early structures, built because of lumber scarcity in the region, are still in good condition today. Straw bale buildings have environmental, performance, and economic advantages, compared to wood-frame buildings with fiber glass insulation.

So family and friends arrived at the Echeverrias' at 9 a.m. on this particular "barn-raising" morning, and by two in the afternoon, where once only stood uprights and a roof, there stood a home ready for windows, doors, and stucco. The bales were placed on a special foundation and stacked just as if they were Lego blocks, with special crews to create eighth, quarter, and half bales.

Once the bales were placed, the next step was to wrap the walls in chicken wire held in place with baling twine (special needles were created to sew the wire to the bales). Finally, stucco was applied to the exterior, while adobe plaster was used on the interior walls. The inside was framed out just like every other house.

To celebrate after a long day of stacking, the Echeverrias, sheep herders, hosted a lamb barbeque with cold beer and iced tea for all the participants. The food and fellowship made the hard day's work more than worth the effort.

A modern-day barn raising brings about community in a neighborhood that might lose sight of the act of neighborliness. Bonds form when people do projects together, and a lifetime of stories are created. ❧

10

Obtain a copy of Barbara Mandrell & George Jones' version of 'I Was Country When Country Wasn't Cool'

(written by Kye Fleming & Dennis Morgan, charted Country #No. 1 in 1981).

No one sings it like Barbara Mandrell. Even if you were never really country, you sure feel country singing this song along with Barbara. When it first came out I used to belt it out at the top of my lungs — when no one was around, of course. This song struck a cord with so many country and rural folk that it was no surprise it hit the top of the charts. It came out at a time when it was cool to dress "cowboy" whether you were from the country or not; even for the urbanite that loved the country the song made sense.

Imagine "I Was Hip Hop When Hip Hop Wasn't Cool" or "I Was Baggy-Pants Dressed When Baggy-Pants Dressed Wasn't Cool". These songs just don't cut it.

So many country music stars today are cross-over. While jazz or classical might be your music of choice, just a sprinkle of country will set the mood if you're striving for that country feeling. And today's country music doesn't always carry the twangy tone that for some is a bit over the top. Discover your favorite country singer by sampling today's large selection of contemporary country music.

MY PERSONAL LIST

My Favorite Country Songs

☐ _____

☐ _____

☐ _____

☐ _____

☐ _____

☐ _____

☐ _____

☐ _____

☐ _____

☐ _____

☐ _____

☐ _____

☐ _____

☐ _____

☐ _____

11

Stargaze.

On cool, fall nights Dad would take us outside on the farm to look up at a moonless sky to hunt for the Big and Little Dippers. As we got older we were shown other constellations, too. City lights can dim the magical night sky, but your own telescope can make up for what city lights might obscure.

Using one of his powerful set of binoculars mounted on a tripod, my bother, Patrick, in the tradition of our father, showed his own children what to look for in the sky. At the time, his three-year-old daughter, McKenzie, asked, "How far away is the moon, Daddy?" After replying that it's quite far away from Arizona, McKenzie replied, "As far away as Kansas?" referencing their annual trek to Kansas to see her mommy's family. It's in these small moments of time that we discover how big creation truly is; the sky is full of wonders. You can go to the Internet to discover what to watch for any night of the week. If you picked July 31st to star gaze you'd discover that the Lagoon Nebula is visible low in the Southern sky on that night. To find it you'd look South around 10 p.m. for Sagittarius, a pattern of stars that forms a teapot. The Lagoon Nebula is visible through a small telescope just above the teapot's spout.

Of course, stargazing is not just a "country thing." But gazing up at the sky out in the middle of nowhere away from the city is a wonder in and of itself. The sky looms so big and clear you feel almost as if you can touch it. Or at least you can behold a good bit of it. The serious stargazer learns that the complex night sky is composed of 88 constellations, most of which are visible throughout the United States at different times of the year. We also discover that on a clear, moonless night, more than a thousand stars are visible. Truly, the myriad of sky-hosted objects visible to the unaided eye is impressive — and overwhelming.

To get started, veteran stargazers suggest that you begin your adventures indoors with a good sky-watching guide or star chart. Next, pick a good viewing spot. As my brother did for his children, your own back yard will do just fine. Then, as you gain experience, escape from city lights into the darkness of the countryside. Find a state park or other safe, accessible spot. And try a night without moonlight, so you can see meteors and the Milky Way. Finally, the only instrument that most beginners need is their eyes. Our eyes can detect subtle variations in brightness, determine the colors and relative temperatures of stars, and track the motions of the moon and planets. ✑

MY PERSONAL LIST

Constellations I Want to Observe

- [ ] _____
- [ ] _____
- [ ] _____
- [ ] _____
- [ ] _____
- [ ] _____
- [ ] _____
- [ ] _____
- [ ] _____
- [ ] _____
- [ ] _____
- [ ] _____
- [ ] _____
- [ ] _____

Obtain CDs with the sounds of nature.

One of my earliest childhood memories is of sleeping on the pullout couch in the living room of our tiny home. Mom would leave the front door open with only the screen door separating us from the outside world. I'd fall asleep listening to the sound of croaking frogs and chirping crickets. You can also fall asleep to the gentle sound of waves lapping onto rocks and sweeping across sandy beaches on a remote shoreline — all from a CD for just $14.95. For country themes stick with chirping birds, chirping crickets, and croaking frogs. I'm waiting for them to come out with the mooing cows and baaing sheep. Oh, they have them. Well where was I? And, of course, some sounds of rural life are just not appropriate.

When doing a search on "nature sounds" on the Internet, the bird lover can hear the high-pitched chirp of an Osprey. But my favorite sound of nature comes from the Red-tailed Hawk. Or, if your preference is listening to the haunting howling of a lone wolf, you can find those sounds recorded, too. The National Park Service, in its nature and science section describes natural ambient sounds as "the natural sounds, and their acoustic properties, that exist in a park in the absence of any human-produced noise." Ditch the CD for $14.95 to hear the sounds of nature and instead go on a camping trip, visit a national park, or simply take a walk in the woods.

Farms generate all sorts of natural sounds. Shall I say more? Neighbor friends of ours from the city watched and heard one of our horses race off down the field while snorting and farting the entire run. They'd never heard such a combination of sounds all at once and laughed themselves silly. My brothers and I laughed at them laughing. We were accustomed to such noises. I especially was living with three brothers (I'm writing this book so they can't defend themselves, nor tell stories on me.)

13

Decorate a room in country or cowboy motif
(Especially since it's easy to find the props.)

Mom and Dad's living room is themed in cowboy country and flared with cowboy accents that bring a modern sophistication to this time-honored design. You'll find the "Murphree" brands in a brass pot with some of Dad's homemade rib-cacti walking sticks. Mom's saddle that she used when riding in the Quadrille de Mujeres — a women's drill team on horses — is regally stationed in the corner near a plant. The finishing touch highlights an antique round coffee table positioned over a cow hide. Plus, a variety of Spanish and decorative crosses strategically placed on the wall above the leather couch tops it all off.

You'll find countless resources to guide you as you decorate using a rural or country theme. The trick is to study a variety of furniture catalogues and decorating guides to find out what's "in" and what's "out." But ultimately, look for what you really like and then design to your own tastes with some decorative props you might have in storage or that can easily be found by shopping around. An old pair of cowboy boots can be the bowl anchor for a center piece. Or, that old wall phone stuck in the corner of your attic might serve as a conversational piece in your country décor.

MY PERSONAL LIST

My Decorative Plans

- [ ] _____
- [ ] _____
- [ ] _____
- [ ] _____
- [ ] _____
- [ ] _____
- [ ] _____
- [ ] _____
- [ ] _____
- [ ] _____
- [ ] _____
- [ ] _____
- [ ] _____
- [ ] _____
- [ ] _____

14

Invest in a few country decorating books.

Mom has several decorating books that suit her taste and style. She referenced these books as she planned how she was going to decorate her living room. Often, leafing through them gives her new ideas for her decorating efforts around the house.

Some of the decorating books are so beautifully laid out that they become perfect coffee-table books and thus part of the decor. When I redid my own house I picked up one reference guide that featured the Tuscan Farmhouse look. Additionally, I looked for decorating guides that catered to late Victorian as my bedroom furniture is antique from the late Queen Victoria era.

As Americans relocate all over the country, one current population wave is washing up right here in the Southwest. Here, you can "cowboy up!" If you're from the East coast and want to transplant your region's tastes, by all means do. However, if you're a recent fan of the contemporary country look, start with a fresh creative canvas and amaze yourself with what you can do. The country or western-style decorating books will be your trusted resource.

MY PERSONAL LIST

My Decoration Plans

- [ ] _____
- [ ] _____
- [ ] _____
- [ ] _____
- [ ] _____
- [ ] _____
- [ ] _____
- [ ] _____
- [ ] _____
- [ ] _____
- [ ] _____
- [ ] _____
- [ ] _____
- [ ] _____
- [ ] _____

15

Subscribe to a country living or rural life magazine.

One of my favorite magazines to flip through is Country Home quickly found at www.countryhome.com. And, of course, other publications cater to country life, rural living, and agriculture. Our family forever subscribed to Cotton Farming. Roam the Internet to find the publication that suits your fancy and subscribe. Even as décor for you coffee table, certain publications can add flair to the environment you're working to achieve.

At the most, a monthly country living magazine will feed you with regular "how to" tips to satisfy your desire for the country life. One of my favorite sections in Country Home is a department called "The Nest." This department gives tips on home décor, style showcases, and much more.

Style magazines are ideal for staying updated or simply getting new ideas. Select those decorating tips in a magazine that suit your taste. The idea is to let these publications inspire and drive your creativity. ❧

Blow up and frame old photos of country or rural life.

So many of us have some connection to country or rural life. Even if we didn't grow up on a farm we might have worked summers on one. All my cousins can attest to their summers on the farm with my family. Though every one of them grew up in the city or suburbs, in the summer they spent several weeks with my brothers and me. Surely during those special times that you spent in the country you might have snapped a photo or two. One special black and white photo I have of my Dad is him as a little boy holding a chicken and sitting on a rusty old bench. In a similar fashion, I have a photo of Mom as a little girl feeding the chickens on her grandparent's farm. They are picture perfect to me.

Such family photos can become fashionable wall accessories in your home. Some photos literally take on a fine art quality to them especially if restored and correctly matted and framed.

17

Use country scents around your home.

Today's modern fabric scents and scented candles can mimic some of the most wonderful fragrances of the country (while making sure they don't mimic the worst scents of country life).

I remember crawling between freshly washed and line-dried bed sheets and snuggling in deep. They were always comfortable and smelled so clean. Mom and Dad would tuck us in tight, give us a kiss, and turn out the lights.

My favorite "clean sheets" fragrance is from Lysol called Crisp Linen®. I spray the scent on the mattress before I make up the bed with clean sheets and then spray the Crisp Linen® over the newly made bed.

With a search on the Internet you can run into candle country and harvest scents with names like Autumn Breezes, Autumn Sunrise, Butter Nut Crunch, Country Fireplace, Fall Breeze, Fall Sunset and Fall Pine.

With your favorite country fragrance gracing your linens, bury your face in your clean, fresh pillow each night and breathe deep before slumber. Or, hunt for a favorite candle scent and light it up. Remember when lighting candles to always snuff them out when you leave the room.

18

Join 4-H as a leader.

4-H, the largest non-formal U.S. youth development program, began as a way of involving the heads, hearts, health, and hands of farm youth in practical, hands-on education in agriculture- and home economics-related subjects relevant to their everyday lives. In 2002, 4-H celebrated its centennial. According to 4-H headquarters, early programs tied both public and private resources together for the purpose of helping rural youth. All three of my brothers and I went through 4-H while growing up on the farm in Arizona. Involve your own children if they're interested. Since the modern-day 4-H message states, "4-H is a community of young people across America who are learning leadership, citizenship and life skills" it doesn't matter where you live.

4-H began to extend into urban areas in the 1950s. Later, the basic 4-H focus became the personal growth of the member. Life skills development was built into 4-H projects, activities and events to help youth become contributing, productive, self-directed members of society. The organization changed in the 1960s, combining 4-H groups divided by gender or race into a single integrated program. Also in the 1960s, more than half of 4-H participants were non-farm youth. Today, 43 percent are from rural areas and towns of up to 10,000; 57 percent then are from larger cities, their suburbs, and from large inner cities. Thirty one percent of 4-H'ers are from racial and ethnic minorities.

The 4-H program combines the cooperative efforts of nearly 7 million youth and more than 500,000 volunteer leaders. One could be you. Additionally, 105 state land-grant universities, state and local governments, private-sector partners, state and local 4-H foundations, the National 4-H Council, the National 4-H Headquarters in the Cooperative State Research and the Education and Extension Service (CSREES) of the U.S. Department of Agriculture work in concert to advance and celebrate our youth.

And finally, 4-H programs are conducted in 3,051 counties of the United States, the District of Columbia, Puerto Rico, Virgin Islands, Guam, American Guam, American Samoa, Micronesia, and Northern Mariana Islands. 4-H alumni now total about 60 million. 4-H-type programs are truly international, with 4 million youth in more than 60 countries in similar programs.

So join the crowd, and make a difference in the lives of our most valuable resource — youth.

Become a financial supporter of FFA.

There is no greater organization for learning leadership, speaking, and developing organizational skills. Participating in FFA is a Murphree tradition: My three brothers and I were in the Future Farmers of America and both my Dad and I were chapter treasurers for our respective chapters. Dad can still recite the Treasurer's creed. I earned my state farmer pin.

Organized as the "Future Farmers of America" in 1928 in Kansas City, Missouri, the official organization name was changed to The National FFA Organization in 1988 to reflect the broadening field of agriculture, which today encompasses more than 300 careers in everything from agri-science to biotechnology to turf grass management. In 1950, Congress granted FFA a federal charter, making it an integral, intra-curricular part of public agricultural instruction under the National Vocational Education Acts. FFA operates on local, state and national levels. Student members belong to chapters organized at the local school level. Agricultural education instructors serve as chapter advisors. Chapters are organized under state associations headed by an advisor and executive secretary, often employees of the state department of education. States conduct programs and host annual conventions.

20

Travel to a farm.

Until we grew up, my three brothers and I didn't really appreciate our life on an Arizona cotton farm. As a child, growing up takes too long and we were ready to go big time in the big city. But it didn't take long for us to realize what we really had.

During my early career years as a journalist, I participated in Project CENTRL; a two-year leadership training program geared toward people who live and work in rural areas. Sponsored by the University of Arizona, classmates each had to pick a project close to the end of the training to contribute something to their area. I decided to do something for the Phoenix area Boys and Girls Club. My project was to bring young inner-city children out to visit farms. I connected with the local farmers I knew and took a group of children to different types of farm operations.

Today, farms throughout the United States cater to the uninitiated city or suburban dweller. Some are so popular that they're generating nearly as healthy revenues by catering directly to the public in produce sales and/or sale of farm tours than actual farming. So much can be learned in such a short time by visiting a working farm. What surprises most is the diversity of farming. Farms today bust the stereotypes.

21

Read the Little House series by Laura Ingalls Wilder.

Even if you have already read them, reread the series (rereading a classic is a rediscovery). Every generation of little girls has read this series since the first book was published in 1932. I received my first Laura Ingalls Wilder book when I was eight, and after each one I was ready to read the next in the series. The Ingalls Wilder books actually inspired me to become a writer and ultimately a journalist. Laura's words about her life growing up in a new and growing country in the late 1800s comes alive as clearly and crisply today as I'm sure the telling of the stories came alive to Laura when she began writing about her childhood. And while you can almost hear Pa's fiddle play and imagine the fearsome cold of the The Long Winter, it makes you appreciate the comforts of our modern-day world.

The next generation in our family is rediscovering this series as my sister-in-law reads the books to her girls. They learn about life in rural America in the 1860s and 1870s and can then compare that with their lives today.

MY PERSONAL LIST

My Favorite Laura Ingalls Wilder Books

☐ _____

☐ _____

☐ _____

☐ _____

☐ _____

☐ _____

☐ _____

☐ _____

☐ _____

☐ _____

☐ _____

☐ _____

☐ _____

☐ _____

☐ _____

22

Read Rebecca of Sunnybrook Farm.

Another classic, this book, too, captures the feel of rural life. When Rebecca Rowena Randall goes to live with her spinster aunts in Riverboro, they find her to be more of a handful than they bargained for. But even more surprising than the transition of Rebecca into a well-mannered young lady are the effects that Rebecca has on her aunts' humdrum lives. Rebecca, with her wide dark eyes and spirit, will change their lives — and the lives of everyone she meets — forever.

Other children's classics to consider include Willa Cather's O! Pioneers or My Antonia, and Mark Twain's Adventures of Huckleberry Finn and Tom Sawyer.

MY PERSONAL LIST

My List of Books That Take Me Back to the Country

- ☐ _____
- ☐ _____
- ☐ _____
- ☐ _____
- ☐ _____
- ☐ _____
- ☐ _____
- ☐ _____
- ☐ _____
- ☐ _____
- ☐ _____
- ☐ _____
- ☐ _____
- ☐ _____
- ☐ _____

23

Read Zane Grey Novels.

Are you a Zane Gray fan? Then you probably have most of his books and know that to read his novels is to enter a different time. Periodically, Mom will have one of Grey's novels tucked under her arm, heading to her cozy library to sit in an overstuffed chair with a lap blanket to get immersed in *Riders of the Purple Sage*.

If you want to become an aficionado of the Western novel, then you should try one or more of these three great classics; Jack Schaefer's *Shane*, Owen Wister's *The Virginian* and Zane Grey's *Riders of the Purple Sage*.

24

Ride a horse.

We forgot our boots, but couldn't pass up the ride. Julie, Brent and Pat Murphree.

Even in major metropolitan areas, it won't take you long to find where horses are boarded for pleasure riding. My first horse was Lattada. She was Arabian and Shetland and very strong willed. But Lattada was my dream horse. After reading *Black Beauty* as a child, my big dream was to own my own horse. My brothers and I all learned how to ride on her and spent many a lazy summer morning brushing, leading her around, and saddling her up for a ride. From her, we've had many horses since, including Mom's quarter horses for her drill work in the Quadrille de Mujeres. Some of our dearest moments involved our horses. All this considering the fact that I am allergic to horses! Love is blind, especially when my eyes would nearly swell shut from my reaction to the horse dander. Go figure.

It's typical for an expecting mare to have her filly or colt at night when no one's around to see, just a little morning surprise out in the pasture. But one special event involved nearly the entire family watching the birth of Gin Dusky Brooks. Ginger, the mare, was Mom's Quadrille horse. From then on we were attached to Gin Dusky and her to us.

Horse people will tell you that horses teach responsibility, help you develop skills beyond riding, and show you the same depth of loyalty as your dog. While they can be quite an investment, I've never heard anyone say they regret having their horses. 🐎

Buy a cowboy hat, then head to the rodeo.

For a rodeo, don't ever forget your cowboy hat. Julie and Brent Murphree.

Because of Mom's participation in the Quadrille de Mujeres, our family attended nearly a dozen rodeos a year. You won't feel dorky wearing a cowboy hat when you attend a rodeo; just make sure you're wearing boots along with your hat and not Nike tennis shoes.

The well-worn hats are my favorite. I used to take my grandpa's hat and wear it. When Dad tossed an old one to the closet shelf, my older brother, Brent, and I would retrieve it for our cowboy outfits. All our family pictures taken when my brothers and I were young show us in droopy, oversized cowboy hats. My baby brother, Curt, was never without a hat, either. Today, he's Mr. Sophisticated businessman.

26

Go to a western store.

Show off your cowboy boots even when playing Army with your brother. Brent and Julie Murphree.

To obtain the cowboy hat you need go to a western wear store. If you can't find a store near you, go online to obtain a catalogue or simply shop the Internet. A slow cruise through a local western store will reveal all sorts of wardrobe features in the style of the traditional cowboy or cowgirl. My favorite section to check out was always the cowboy boots. I used to wear my older brother's boots until Mom bought me my own pair of black boots. Running after the older cousins in a pair of oversized boots didn't get me very far very fast.

Another reason it's fun to shop in a western store is the smell of leather, especially for boot, belt, or saddles. Some stores serve as both a western wear and feed store. In these stores you'll find a line-up of freshly tooled saddles.

Though Mom had at least three saddles, she never passed the saddle section without checking out the new arrivals. One visit prompted her to saddle up on a brand new saddle with silver trim. She forgot that the saddle stand displaying the saddle is a lot less stable than a horse and went crashing to the floor in front of the store owner. Dad had fun with that story the entire day. He would say, "Mom prided herself in never being bucked off a horse, but the one that got her was an in-store saddle stand." Cowgirls have to try on a saddle just like trying on a pair of pants.

Western-style wear comes and goes for the general public but serves as every day wear for the true cowboy and cowgirl.

And the true cowboy loves his gear. To protect the innocent — actually the mischievously creative — I won't name names, but a story is told about one cowboy in quite the frisky mood gently tapping his slumbering wife on the shoulder saying, "Hello cowgirl…." Opening her eyes and looking up at her husband through a sleepy gaze she sees him with nothing on but his leather chaps and a smile on his face. ✤

27

Attend a tractor pull.

Yes, there is also a National Tractor Pullers Association (NTPA). One year, Mom and I were asked to set up our cotton booth at a local tractor pulling event in Yuma, Arizona, to promote and highlight all the uses of cotton in consumer products. You'll find as dedicated of an audience going to tractor pulls as you do attending the symphony. Vintage tractors from all makes, models and years are a regular highlight at a tractor pull. If new to this type of event, what strikes the novice is the power in the mechanical beast.

The NTPA was established in 1969 by representatives from eight states (Illinois, Indiana, Iowa, Michigan, Minnesota, Missouri, Ohio, and Pennsylvania). They established the rules that give the sport structure. For more than 36 years they've been the premier sanctioning body of truck and tractor pulling.

One highlight for many attendees includes the vintage tractors on display. Hunt for the roped-off display and watch the older generation look with longing and remembrance at an earlier era. Be bold enough to ask someone if they grew up on a farm and what tractors they drove, and learn a little more about farm life.

You can go to the NTPA's Web site at www.ntpapull.com to learn more. ❧

28

Go to the county fair.

The county fair was an annual event for our family. Here, we would show our 4-H (see No. 18 "Join 4-H as a Leader") beef or swine each year, and then at the end of the fair sell the animal at market. The money we made off of our 4-H project went into our savings accounts where we saved up for either next year's 4-H project or earmarked our profit for something fun. One year I used part of the money I made from my 4-H project, as well as what I earned chopping weeds in our cotton fields, to visit my Uncle in Hawaii.

The county fair was a time to meet up with friends, practice our showmanship, learn about market prices, and just have fun. The variety of animals — from rabbits in the small animal barn to steers — was a way to learn all about animals and how to care for them. We often had so much fun hanging out with our other 4-H friends we didn't even bother with the rides.

I'll always be partial to the county fair. I had my first boyfriend crush during the 4-H county fair. We both had swine projects. And you ask, what was my pick up line? "I'll show you my pig if you show me yours?" That wasn't exactly what I said but we did admire each other's 4-H project and talked a lot about how neat it would be to raise horses on a farm (pig farms didn't seem as romantic).

29

Go to the state fair.

It's the same idea here at the state fair but on a much grander scale. In fact, our first experiences at the state fair were a bit more intimidating. To get the rural/country fair feel make sure the animal barns are your first stop.

In fact, stay away from the midway; you'll save money and ensure you retain that good ole country feeling. While there, step in some fresh manure for effect. Just make sure you rinse off before stepping back into your SUV, unless you want that country smell to stay with you a while longer. 🐾

Make the most of harvest time.

My favorite time of year is the fall. In Arizona it means you're finally getting a break from the heat. But for me, it's all the social activities, holidays, and the excitement of harvest time. Arizona cotton farmers typically begin cotton picking season in late September. Everyone and everything buzzes with activity.

At summer's end, the avid gardener is often so overwhelmed by his or her fresh supply of produce that often there aren't enough neighbors to whom to give it away. With the rest it's a time to cook bountiful meals full of fresh-harvested vegetables. The building blocks of a harvest feast from your own garden can include tomatoes, corn, eggplant, summer squash, cucumbers, peppers, and fresh herbs. Also on the list are summer fruits such as watermelon, cantaloupe, and peaches. You might even try to connect with a farm family that's in the midst of harvesting to see how they harvest certain crops.

To begin setting the stage for fall harvest time, decorate your table with yellow and gold. What better colors to usher in the new season and especially Halloween. Fill vases with large, fresh, yellow flowers like sunflowers (from your own garden, tip No. 1). Even the menu you plan for your meals can spell harvest with such foods as pumpkin soup, corn on the cob, and casserole dishes.

Then make sure you plan family activities that celebrate harvest by visiting a farmers' market (tip No. 32), going to a pumpkin patch (tip No. 2) and hosting a harvest celebration. One way I begin to adjust to the change of season is hosting a chili dinner with cornbread and cold beer. Turn the television on to a football game, and it just feels like fall is around the corner.

MY PERSONAL LIST

Harvest Activities for the Year

- ☐ _____
- ☐ _____
- ☐ _____
- ☐ _____
- ☐ _____
- ☐ _____
- ☐ _____
- ☐ _____
- ☐ _____
- ☐ _____
- ☐ _____
- ☐ _____
- ☐ _____
- ☐ _____
- ☐ _____

31

Learn to square dance, country swing or line dance.

During our busy social days as 4-Hers, my brother and I would be busy with our 4-H buddies doing all sorts of fun stuff, including going to dances. One experience was winning a country swing contest with my brother. Who would have thought? I have always said I'm more coordinated in water (we were competitive swimmers growing up) than on land. So when my older brother talked me into competing I cynically looked at him. He replied, "Julie, if you just follow my lead — something hard for you to do, I know — we'll win." And we did!

Just put one foot in front of the other. Well, it's a bit more complicated than that. But today's square dance clubs are not just for country folk anymore. Everyone can square dance, and just about everyone does.

Okay, so square dancing is a bit stale for you. How about learning to country swing? Country swing is now a category within the popular ball room dancing arena and has a huge following.

And then there's the ever popular line dance. No better way to dance with a group when you don't have a partner than to line dance. Line dances today have become more intricate and full of all sorts of fun and flowing moves.

So many cowboys — and cowgirls — I know can dance. Maybe it's their romantic side that gets them out there on the dance floor — or, maybe it's the beer with the country music blaring. Yeah, it's the beer. ✑

32

Shop at a farmer's market.

If you don't participate in a community or urban garden, at least go to a farmers' market for fresh produce, which is laid out and in the open just like old times. You'll often find homemade jams and jellies and other home-grown items that are unique to the specific farmers' market. After one trip you can be sure your food pantry will become a unique assortment of home-grown flavors, thanks to the farmers' market.

Today, across the country, you can find a farmers' market within driving distance. Most crop up over the weekend and are back the following weekend. For specialty farm produce, the farmers' market is perfect. For organic foods, you'll have greater prospects at a farmers' market, though today's supermarkets are improving on the varieties of organic foods they provide. ✤

MY PERSONAL LIST

Farmers' Market Shopping List

- [ ] _____
- [ ] _____
- [ ] _____
- [ ] _____
- [ ] _____
- [ ] _____
- [ ] _____
- [ ] _____
- [ ] _____
- [ ] _____
- [ ] _____
- [ ] _____
- [ ] _____
- [ ] _____
- [ ] _____

Watch old westerns.

Over at Mom and Dad's one night, we sat down with Dad to a rerun of "Gunsmoke." While not initially interested, I was so drawn into the folksy dialogue and the straight-shooting character of Sheriff Matt Dillon that when the show ended I was sad to see the credits come up. Or, how about an old "The Andy Griffith Show" rerun that makes you cry? Classics like "The Cowboys," "High Noon," "Butch Cassidy and the Sundance Kid," "The Man Who Shot Liberty Valance," "The Wild Bunch," "The Searchers," "Unforgiven," "The Good," "The Bad and the Ugly," "RedRiver," and "Stagecoach" put you in a place and time where you wanted to strap on your own six-shooter and ride off into the sunset.

It's easy to find these westerns on Turner Classics and other stations that cater to the old standbys.

Find out what crops grow in your state.

Growing up on an Arizona cotton farm, I assumed everyone knew that Arizona grew cotton. But, even today, when I tell acquaintances where I grew up they are surprised to discover that cotton grows in Arizona. And they're from Arizona! Arizona actually has an interesting variety of food and economic factors. When local economists or tourism professionals promoted the state they spoke of the five "C's" for Arizona: copper, cotton, citrus, climate, and cattle.

Discovering the variety of food commodities in your state becomes a pleasant surprise for nearly everyone. This is a great educational outlet for your children if you assign them the task of discovering what foods and other agricultural commodities their state grows.

Your state grows cranberries? Discover how to raise them and then discover how much that commodity impacts your state's economy. Then go out and buy some cranberry juice. I'm thirsty already.

MY PERSONAL LIST

My State's Crops

- [ ] _____
- [ ] _____
- [ ] _____
- [ ] _____
- [ ] _____
- [ ] _____
- [ ] _____
- [ ] _____
- [ ] _____
- [ ] _____
- [ ] _____
- [ ] _____
- [ ] _____
- [ ] _____

35

Adopt a farm family.

Though off the farm for several years now, I still feel connected to the farm families of my youth and attempt to stay in touch with them as much as I can. If you live near a rural area and meet a farm family, ask if you can start up a periodic email correspondence with them.

This is especially fun for children that might need to interview a farmer for one of their class projects where they're learning about agriculture (see No. 44). One year, the Arizona Science Center asked me to coordinate a "Cotton Day" that they hosted in their newly opened facilities in downtown Phoenix. My network of agriculture contacts jumped at the chance to tell their stories to the general public about farming and the rural life. Our "Talk to a Farmer" station at the Arizona Science Center was one of the most popular stations. We also featured a station where children could plant their own cotton seed or separate cotton lint from seed using a mini cotton gin.

36

Attend and/or participate in a cow-pie throwing contest.

The cow chip — also known as the cow pie, meadow muffin, or pasture patty — is a dried-out, disc-shaped bovine dropping that fuels the competitive spirit among a handful of heartland town folks. Farm-town officials in places like Tilden, Nebraska, and elsewhere bet on cow-chip throwing contests to draw tourists.

While my brothers and I didn't throw pasture patties (as we would have been aiming them at each other), we did have dirt-clod throwing contests. And yes, they eventually were aimed at live targets instead of an imaginary measuring marker. While I can say today I'd probably still rather be hit in the head with a dirt clod lobbed at me by one of my brothers, I'm sure a pasture patty with a moist center would have been more gentle on the temple.

More than a dozen towns throughout the Mid-west (more bovine droppings out there) host annual cow-chip tossing contests. In Prairie du Sac, Wisconsin, for example, townspeople and thousands of tourists line the streets for the tournament of Chips Parade. Beaver, Oklahoma claims the first organized competition in 1970 during the town's annual spring festival. Their "I Flung Dung" T-shirts would have been appropriate for my brothers and I to wear when we tossed horse poop at each other in our more abusive moments.

Yup, they even have a world record for the meadow muffin toss: 185 feet, 5 inches. But some claim the farthest a meadow muffin has ever soared is actually 248 feet — nearly the length of a football field. I knew poop could fly or hit the fan well, but wow!

Simply plug "Cow-Pie Throwing Contests" or "Cow Chip Championships" into Google or Yahoo, and you'll find various locations hosting an event near you. You might even want to participate as a chip-throwing contestant. Warm up the arm beforehand though; you'll want the chip to really go airborne. For the veteran, a good warm up avoids "Poop Elbow." ✍

37

Wear cotton.

It's natural, cool, and comfortable. Take the traditional cowboy and/or farmer. You won't find one manmade fiber on his body. Let's start with the boxers or briefs (I like a guy in briefs, but boxers are cute, too). All cotton. Most farmers and ranchers also will wear an undershirt. All cotton. Out in the elements they sweat, so a cool breeze through their breathable cotton serves as a natural air conditioner. For pants they'll be wearing either Levi's or Wrangler jeans. All cotton. For their shirts, whatever their preferred style, it will be all cotton. The word, then, is wear cotton!

No, you don't have to dress like a farmer. But when putting together your wardrobe for the season look for mix- and-match garments that have natural fibers. Or at least look for a good blend. Even if it's the lesser percentage in the fabric blend, cotton gives the garment its character.

I used to start presentations about fashion and cotton by describing how cotton is so versatile that we wear and use it from cheek to cheek: In the morning momma may use a cotton ball to do her cleansing routine and apply cosmetics and, later, after bathing the baby, dry, wrap, and snuggle it in an all-cotton towel. 🕊

38

Do denim.

If you wear cotton fabrics you probably have quite a bit of denim in your closet. Denim is so comfortable and such an American brand. It took me a while to be able to wear my first pair of Levi's 501 Original jeans, since I was very skinny as a little girl. I was so proud of that first pair that I wore holes in the knees and seat before I gave them up, and even then I didn't toss them. Ask me for them today and I'll pull them out to show you. What's that? No, I can't wear them anymore.

Denim, as with so many other products, emerged because of a huge need and interest in the market. Says Stephen Yafa in his book, *Big Cotton*, "Your denims were jeans, your jeans were blue, so you wore blue jeans and that was that. Strauss quickly realized that pants were more comfortable than overalls, also that people formed a curiously intimate relationship with their denims, much like the affection they developed for a pet. There was a reason. As blue jeans become more pliable through laundering, they caressed areas of the body they initially clutched." I can't say it better!

39

Cook an old-fashioned country meal.

Can you recall a true country meal? Mine would be fried chicken, mashed potatoes and gravy, with green beans. I can taste it even now. Mom makes the best chicken gravy. And by the way, fried chicken is consistently named one of the top five comfort foods. But there are other favorites. Gravy and mashed potatoes are the cornerstone dishes for many country-style meals.

Numerous comfort food rankings exist but you'll nearly always find fried chicken at the top of the list along with chocolate chip cookies, hot chocolate with marshmallows, Jell-O, chili, and chicken soup. Notice that several of these choices might not make your diet list, however. When it comes to your strict comfort food list, health sometimes is helped by a good bowl of chicken soup. My Aunt Sandy says, "When a comfort food is necessary for the soul on special occasions it then becomes health food."

If you are really ambitious in the kitchen and trying to capture that country flavor and aroma, can fresh jellies and jams. Though more goes into canning fresh jellies and jams, the kitchen is a centerpiece for country life. ✧

40

Plant a tree.

One of my favorite trees I planted when I was a child was a cherry tree. The little tree didn't do well at all under the baking Arizona sun. Okay, though I'm a farm kid my green thumb suffers. It doesn't hurt to select a tree variety that thrives in the right climate. Despite my poor selection of a tree variety, the idea of planting, growing and caring for my own tree was exciting. Dad later showed me how easily the native trees of Arizona thrive and require less water, which is a key concern when planting in our arid state. This includes from the shrubby Palo Verde to the acacia tree. The Ajo oak and the Gooding ash are other examples of trees that are also unique to Arizona.

The National Arbor Day Foundation tells us that trees around your house can increase your property value by 15 percent. Plus, the trees you plant remove CO_2 from the air, produce oxygen, and give birds a home. I also learned that shade trees planted east and west of your home can cut cooling costs by 15 to 35 percent. And the experts remind us that flowering trees serve as food for wildlife. A Desert Willow in my backyard is a favorite with visiting hummingbirds.

If you join the National Arbor day Foundation you get 10 trees free. At www.arborday.org you can even learn how to properly prune your trees. ✎

41

Explore your family history.

Siblings can get excited about their family heritage, especially when they discover that their ancestors grew up on a farm too.
Julie with her brothers –
Patrick (on the saddle), Brent and Curt.

Find out if any of your ancestors were farmers. Since 98 percent of the American population farmed during the early years of this country it's a safe bet that you have a farmer or two in your family background. Mom's been researching our family history for several years now, and on either side of the family tree she found agriculture families settling throughout the country to raise family and crops and carve out a life in untamed and unbroken lands.

When I lost my first grandparent as a teenager, family history began to really interest me. It might have been a way to hold on to the grandpa I'd just lost to his life graduation (my term I coined several years ago to avoid using the dreary word funeral). As Mom uncovered more fascinating ancestors on our family tree and we then mutually discovered snippets of the way they lived, I felt we were putting the pieces together of a huge family puzzle.

As a leisure pursuit, genealogy is one of the country's fastest-growing hobbies. Filling in names and dates on the family tree becomes a worthwhile goal when you want to uncover your past.

42

Plan your vacation to take your family history one step further.

The best part of family outings is the hiking and exploring. Julie with her Dad, Pat, hiking around Arizona.

Yes, uncovering your genealogy is worthwhile, but doing a little field research is even more exciting. If you discover the agrarian side to your family tree, take the leap and turn it into a family vacation. Spending a few days among your people and surrounding yourself with the food, music, stories, and celebrations that have shaped your family in large and small ways will add so much to your kin.

Mom had discovered a relative of ours that grew up in the Southeast in the 1800s. So on my back-and-forth work trips to Birmingham, Alabama, I went to where my ancestor farmed, raised his family, and was eventually shot by an assassin who didn't approve   of his support and sympathies toward the recently "Freedman" after Lincoln's emancipation proclamation. I was able to find Grandpa Crossland's gravesite, cabin (now a historical landmark), and even the bloodstained floorboards where he bled to death after the shooting.

Families can sort through church records and provincial archives, drive down picturesque country roads, and visit with local people. You not only discover who your agrarian ancestors are, but something about how they lived, and how the historical events of the day impacted their lives. It's that understanding that makes your vacation rich in tradition, heritage, and remembrance.

Some families even travel to the National Archives in Washington to learn more about additional family details. Two sides to the National Archives and Records Administration (NARA) exist. The National Archives Experience, the public side of the agency, helps citizens connect to the nation's past. In the Archives Building's famous Rotunda for the Charters of Freedom, you can see for yourself the documents that began it all: the original Declaration of Independence, the Constitution, and the Bill of Rights. Beyond the Rotunda, far from the public eye, the Archives is a vital resource for scholars and government agencies, preserving our past and present in a labyrinth of stacks and storage nooks. The new Public Vaults exhibit gives visitors the sense of exploring the Archives through a collection of original documents, video and audio recordings, and new interactive exhibits. A Learning Center (opened fall 2005) further expands NARA's public educational mission. Mom and I planned a visit to the National Archives one year while attending a leadership trip in Washington D.C. Visiting the other part of the Archives was like walking into a vault full of our past.

Every family is a part of history, not only of the big events of their day but also those personal histories of triumphs and tragedies. And remember that genealogy is not just about the dead, the passing on of genes, or sorting through dusty archives. It also involves the living people you meet along the way. For me, this involved meeting a direct descendent of M.T. Crossland when I went to discover more about my Great Grandpa from Alabama. In fact, for everyone who has taken a genealogical journey there is a story about a living relative, a librarian, a courthouse clerk, a farmer — all strangers — who helped them in their quest. ❧

43

Help a teacher with Ag in his/her classroom.

Beyond the classroom setting I had 4-H and FFA growing up, so if I wasn't living the agriculture lifestyle I was learning about it. Today, through an organization called Agriculture in the Classroom, a more concerted effort to teach agriculture to young people exists. Go to www.agclassroom.org to check out the organization.

Though today we might not realize it, agriculture and education have been closely linked throughout much of the United States' history. As stated earlier, when most Americans lived on farms or in small towns, students living on farms did farm chores before and after school. As we know, the school year was determined by planting, cultivating, and harvesting schedules. Leaf through the old school books and you'll uncover the detailed agricultural references and examples of farming and farm animals. Agriculture began as a familiar part of nearly every child's life back then.

Ag in the Classroom's Web site tells us that, "In the 1920s, 30s and 40s, the farm population shrank and the emphasis on agricultural decreased in school books and educational materials. Educators then focused on agriculture as an occupational specialty, rather than an integral part of every student's life. Agriculture education was mainly offered to those few students wanting to make a career of agriculture. During this period, a small nucleus of educators and others pushed for more agriculture in education. To them, the role of farming and food and fiber production with environmental quality, including wildlife habitat, clean water, and the preservation and improvement of forests meant that agriculture should be taught in the classroom."

So in 1981 the USDA established Agriculture in the Classroom. The countless agriculture-oriented partnerships that include the National Association of State Department's of Agriculture helped advance the cause of Ag in the Classroom.

Agriculture in the Classroom serves as a refreshing and flexible way to teach children about from where their food and fiber comes. Ag in the Classroom also supplements and enhances the teacher's existing curriculum.

Children will tell you how much fun they have learning about American Agriculture. Parents working in the classroom helping the teachers add that Ag in the Classroom is one of the most interactive times for the children. Parents, too, are the biggest fans.

44

Pick your favorite farm animal and learn about it.

So often girls will pick the horse as their favorite animal, which happens to be my choice as well. As a youngster I read everything I could get my hands on to learn about horses. Then, when Mom and Dad brought home my horse Latada, it was one of the most wonderful experiences of my life growing up on the farm.

The next most popular animal on the farm might be the dog. And, of course, the typical herd dog found on a farm or ranch is one of several breeds of dogs used for herding livestock, including the Belgian sheepdog, Collie, German shepherd, and the Old English sheepdog.

Not to be outdone by the popularity of the horse or the dog, don't forget one of the most well-known farm animals, the bovine. You know, the cow. Arizona is home to a famous steer that "ain't no bull." Tex Earnhardt of Earnhardt Auto Centers, an Arizona icon in his own right, in his signature country drawl spoke the phrase "This Ain't No Bull" while comfortably sitting atop a full-grown steer during his television commercials.

Their "No Bull Since 1951" trademark left a lasting impression on me as a four-year-old child. I remember watching Tex sit on that steer, worrying that he might get gored by the steer's big horns.

So one afternoon when Mom had taken our Ford Mustang in for servicing I walked up to one of the auto mechanics. With a furrowed brow and hands on my hips, in a serious tone I asked, "Is this the place where there ain't no bull?" Surprised, but patiently waiting for the adults' laughter to die down, I insisted on an answer. I don't remember his reply but must have been satisfied because I do recall walking to our car happily licking a grape lollipop.

And let's not forget that a great place for kids to learn about animals is in school. Teachers often teach a curriculum concentrated on animals during their "Ag in the Classroom" segment (see #No. 43) since children are so fascinated with them. My friend, a Kindergarten teacher, hatched chicks in her classroom during her agriculture week with her kids, which is a very popular way to teach agriculture in the classroom.

If you are involved in 4-H, you know that the organization hosts a lot of clubs that feature animals. When growing up, I had friends that had their rabbits and guinea pigs in 4-H besides the more traditional farm animals like beef, swine and lamb. 4-H's animal science program is also very popular with youth. ⌘

45

Visit your local Ag Extension Service.

All our 4-H activities over the years were supported, and backed by our state's agriculture extension service. The extension service still serves as a great resource as an adult.

I can go to an area extension service and pick up all kinds of literature and find just what I need as it relates to gardening, landscaping, and so much more. If you check out an extension service on the Web by topic you will probably be able to find a section on "animals and livestock," "farm management," "food and nutrition," "crops and nursery," "health and safety," "home garden and lawn and landscape," "environment and natural resources," "family," and even "bio-security." If you go into the "animals and livestock" topic you'll see additional links that cover all agriculture farm animal programs and so much more. An interesting one in this section is "4-H programs in animal science."

Our extension service hosted meetings and events for us, including a 4-H dance one year. Additionally, the extension service provided facilities and space for a special Ag Education day for teachers throughout the valley. Your local Ag Extension Service becomes a vital resource for all sorts of activities. Discover the nearest one in your area, and find out what special events they host.

46

Study agriculture in America.

For the past 15 years, Mom and I have been involved with the National Cotton Women's Committee within the National Cotton Council. To pull our presentations, fashion shows, and booths together, we've leaned heavily on the numerous agriculture resources that exist.

You can find resources too numerous to count about agriculture and life in rural America. Besides Web searches, some of the historical novels that focus on the more agrarian period of America's history (see Nos. 21-23) help you understand just what agriculture was and is like in America.

Additionally, the American Farm Bureau serves as a great resource for anyone wanting to learn more about agriculture. At www.fb.org, a wealth of information and insights can be gleaned. The Farm Bureau is local, state, national, and international in its scope and is known as the voice of agriculture at all levels.

MY PERSONAL LIST

Questions I Have About Agriculture

- ☐ _____
- ☐ _____
- ☐ _____
- ☐ _____
- ☐ _____
- ☐ _____
- ☐ _____
- ☐ _____
- ☐ _____
- ☐ _____
- ☐ _____
- ☐ _____
- ☐ _____
- ☐ _____

47

❦❧

Work on a farm or ranch.

Though we had a cotton-pickin' good time on the cotton picker for this family photo years ago, cotton harvest time is hot, dusty work. Clockwise: Pat Murphree, Pennee Murphree, Brent Murphree, Julie Murphree, Curt Murphree and Patrick Murphree.

But only temporarily — the pay is lousy. During the summers, my brothers and I worked on the farm chopping weeds in cotton fields, trimming Pistachio trees in the orchard, spraying weeds on the ditch bank, and anything else Dad assigned us to do. We learned to drive farm equipment early on and spent most of our time outside (to Mom's relief). Though the work was hard and the pay wasn't great, when we reminisce today about life on the farm it's often about some of our summer exploits while working.

One summer I was in charge of our little crew going through the orchard trimming and tying trees to stakes. We ranged in age from 11 to 17, and as the day wore on temperatures soared, we grew hot, and tempers flared. One crew member kept skipping trees or clipping off perfectly grafted buds. So I kept harping on him to watch what he was doing. The oldest member in our crew, Laura, told me not to worry about him, just get my job done. I remember as if it was yesterday saying, "I've worked too damn hard and long in these trees for someone to screw them up now!" Surprising myself and everyone else with what I said, Laura replied back, "You're right!" After that we all proceeded along more carefully to prevent having to go back over and redo our work. What a lesson in doing it right the first time.

Programs exist where you can actually work for a short period on a farm or ranch. Working in the agriculture setting is perfect for teaching the work ethic to teenagers. Today, our farming friends still host friends and relatives' children on the farm. When we were young Mom and Dad might have as many as eight to 10 kids helping us on the farm. ❦

48

Host a party near a country-style landmark.

In the little town in which I grew up, our historical landmarks were not as significant as those in some rural areas throughout America, but we could find our spots of which to be proud. Each year Stagecoach Days was a celebration of Maricopa's history and community.

Today, families can gather at a historical covered bridge landmark to picnic; old, famous statues of war heroes (especially if the statue depicts someone in their family tree); and tour the town's old one-room school house built long ago. Discover nearby landmarks near your home, and set up a family outing.

Nearly every small, rural town has a Founder's Day. If you live near one of those towns but don't know much about their history or events, go to their Web site or Chamber of Commerce and find out what special day they host to celebrate their town. More often than not, agriculture played some part in the town's founding and emergence.

49

Visit a dude ranch.

The work crew of cousins survived the harsh labor to adulthood to laugh and tell stories about it today. From left to right: David Thompson holding Lisa's son Patrick, Geoff Howard, Chad Thompson, Julie Murphree, Brent Murphree, Lisa Thompson Allen, Curt Murphree and Patrick Murphree.

Those who have vacationed at a dude ranch claim it's one of the best vacations a family can experience. Cool, fresh mountain air, open spaces and a spirit of western romance all combine to help you live a common fantasy: Life on the Range. Though my brothers and I lived on a "dirt" farm where agriculture crops were the main commodity, we had relatives in Washington and Oregon where the more "dude ranch" experience took place. Coming from a cattle and ranch family, I remember visiting our relatives out there one summer and simply sitting in the living room staring out their picture window, soaking in the scenery. Then we'd go horseback riding; the feel of a steady horse beneath you as you top the next rise and come upon yet another breathtaking canyon made me feel really small.

The popularity of the dude ranch emerged naturally as most of the American West had been explored by the end of the 1800s. Families running dude ranches will tell you that Easterners sought a respite from the crowded, craziness of fast-paced cities. When "city folk" came to the West to get away, they encountered awesome beauty, adventure and the honest simplicity of the cowboy way of life. Today, city and suburban dwellers come from all over. The Dude Ranchers' Association at www.duderanch.org has more than 120 member ranches in 13 Western states from an original 35 member ranches when it first formed in 1926. Go there to learn about the dude ranch vacation.

Mom and Dad's place became a sort of dude ranch in the summer. But my cousins and friends would insist that our modified dude ranch was anything and everything but a "respite from the craziness of city life."

During the summer, we all worked and worked hard. No one was exempt from the dreaded 4:30 a.m. wake-up call. The entire crew of cousins and friends (often 8 to 10 at a time) were out in the fields with either hoes for chopping weeds in cotton fields or clippers for trimming trees in the tree orchards by 5:00 a.m.

We preferred the pistachio tree orchards. The work was a little more varied and once the trees were full-grown with a canopy of branches we'd gain a bit more shade.

We loved to suggest alternatives to work and even attempted some creative solutions for getting out of work including heat stroke and more. But in the end, Mom and Dad found us out every time. Cousin Geoff headed home after a two-week stay telling his family, "Nothing ever hurts at the Murphree's."

50

Attend church.

Heading for church, only Brent looks like he's really ready and willing to go. Julie, Brent and Patrick Murphree.

Whether Catholic or Protestant, you might identify with going to church (of course, if your memories of Sunday services are not fond ones you have permission to stick to the previous 49 tips; be encouraged though to seek and "ye shall find"). The tie small-town churches have to the local community is typically strong and enduring. In some rural settings townspeople didn't need a community center, since the churches were the community centers. In fact, I remember someone saying the best way to find out about a community was to attend its churches (the good and the bad).

On business or leisure trips that keep me over the weekend, I'll attend the nearest Catholic or Protestant church. It just feels good, even if the liturgy is unfamiliar to me.

In the little dirt-scrabble Maricopa community of my youth, my family attended a non-denominational church that held services in a Quonset hut where it was hotter than h--- in the summer and colder than the Arctic in winter. Legend has it that Maricopa's Community Church originated as a result of the local cotton farmers donating the value of a cotton trailer full of cotton. (For a thorough history on the town of Maricopa, obtain a copy of *Reflections of a Desert Town* by Patricia Brock.) Old wood pews were also donated that happened to be linked together in an entire row. And since the pews were never bolted down to the cement floor, at least one Sunday a month the high school boys (who always sat together) would lean back far enough to force the entire row to topple back with a loud crash. Oh well, the sparsely populated congregation listened to the visiting pastor with greater intent once the toppled pews were set upright.

One of our favorite parts of the service was communion. Since our church couldn't afford a full-time pastor, we received visiting preachers from different protestant denominations. Each one had a different doctrinal style for conducting communion. One Sunday after the communion plate had been blessed and passed, dozens of miniature communion wafers were left in the plate. The visiting pastor, realizing he'd previously blessed the communion, proceeded to eat every remaining wafer. No amount of throat-clearing and coughing could relieve the pastor's dry-mouth agony until someone brought him a Dixie cup full of tap water. The message that day was short and sweet.

My older brother, Brent, remembers the frequently rumbling trains on the tracks directly behind the Quonset hut. If a visiting pastor didn't realize he needed to pause until the train went by, no one in the congregation would be able to hear him, including those in the front pew. This brought new meaning to the phrase, "So what did you hear in church today?"

Our church attendance was so sparse at times that Sunday school grade levels were often merged for one big Bible teaching. Our community church operated like a large, extended family where annual hay rides, river trips, and other special youth activities created a lifelong bond among participating families. I'll never forget our Band of Love choir of boys and girls singing the praise songs of the 1970s; some of the songs clear compositions of the "Jesus Movement" during that time.

When still involved with the youth in the 1980s, Mom and Dad might tell you working with the church youth produced its own set of unexpected challenges. One story Mom recounts involves driving more than 20 miles (remember, it's the country) to drop off some of the children after a day-long mountain bike ride. She pulled up in front of one family's home with instructions not to hit the automatic door locks in the truck doors. Quickly hopping out of the vehicle with keys still in the ignition, Mom pulled bikes, backpacks and water bottles out of the back at the same time the young troupe of kids spilled out of the cab to help. One of the children lingered in the cab to avoid helping and as he jumped out as if on command, hit the door locks then slammed the truck door. Let's just say he never did that again.

For a special Father's Day service the youth even earned the privilege of conducting the Sunday service — mainly since we weren't sure we could get a visiting pastor down to Maricopa on Father's Day anyway. We even wrote a song for our dads to the tune of "Hello Dolly:" "Hello daddies, well, hello daddies; it's so nice to see you back in church again. You're lookin' swell daddies, we can tell daddies, you're still growing, you're still glowin, in Christ, growing strong. We feel the room swaying for we're all praying that we'll see you here each Sunday from now on …open your hearts daddies, it's time for a brand new start daddies … daddies don't ever go away, daddies don't ever go away from Christ." None of us have made it to Nashville, yet.

Which leads me to speak of our farmer dads: Every dad always had unoriginal excuses to farm instead of attending church. Their reasons might include the acoustics in a tin building while a badly out-of-tune upright piano played the traditional hymns or the latest visiting preacher's salvation message to this "wilderness" church was the same as the previous visiting preacher's. So a few guilt-induced work projects the farm dads spearheaded made up for not attending church — no, not because their faith was based on works but because they had spouses to answer to. These projects included "dragging off" the property with a tractor to clear the weeds and building crosses out of wooden posts so visitors could distinguish our "sanctified" Quonset hut from the other two identical ones on either side. Our farmer dads were always there for the special holiday services, including our unique Father's Day program. Watching a carpenter farmer nail a makeshift cross together and pound it into the tough, unyielding ground in front of our little church has left nearly as profound an impression on me as some of those Sunday morning services.

Our little church happened to be a favorite for the wandering drunks who would come in and sit down during a service. It was a place to just sit and rest and be warmed by the presence of others – or the space heater in the corner. They were never turned away, and it was a lesson for we "wee ones." One of our female church leaders (the church was pretty much run by women) knew them by name. Sometimes she had to shoo them out if they got loud or boisterous, but only if they were creating a disturbance.

So if attending a country church to get that "community feeling" is over the top and you recall the familiar quote, "the only thing wrong with churches is there's people in them," I still encourage you to go because of the lives we can share with people in our community! Besides, churchgoers will acknowledge they are "not perfect, just forgiven."

People coming together does mean something, and the numbers confirm it: According to California-based Barna Group, a firm that conducts research about faith in America, more than nine out of 10 American adults engage in some type of faith-related practice during a typical week. The Barna group also says that 45 percent of American adults nationwide attend some type of church service in a typical weekend, not counting a special event such as a wedding or a funeral. Perhaps many do attend to feel grounded, to feel part of a community.

Church, for me, is people. But church is made real with Jesus. Simply Jesus.

My pastor, Gary Kinnaman of Word of Grace in Mesa, Arizona, says, "Jesus plus nothing equals everything." In other words, no rules, no heavy-handed ritual, no works-based excesses, just grace.

It is my relationship with Jesus where he continuously teaches me how to relationship and "do community" with others. Through the Lord's eyes, I'm privileged to look upon another's uniqueness and positively measure the value of their part in helping create community. Apart from him, I cannot completely experience the unconditional depth of his love for me. And, in turn, unconditionally love others.

Remember the familiar old Hymn:

> *Blest be the tie that binds*
> *Our hearts in Christian love.*
> *The fellowship of Kindred minds*
> *Is like to that above*

"The fellowship of kindred minds ..." The phrase summarizes the purpose and the strength of some of the churches in rural communities across America. I do remember part of what I miss so much about my country roots: the coming together, often out of necessity, from diverse backgrounds, to fellowship together in a small church with limited resources. ❧

These 50 tips just scratch the surface. I didn't talk about walks down a country lane, rides in a cotton or hay trailer (not considered safe anymore), adventures frog gigging (hunting for bullfrogs at night), and floats down the river. However, I am hoping these 50 tips inspired your five senses — touch, taste, smell, hear, and see — and helped you capture the full grace of country living.

Let's continue the adventure! Yes, there are countless more ways to experience rural or country life wherever you live. To share your stories, go to www.juliemurphree.com, and we'll exchange stories. Watch for me to post more stories there too!

Epilogue

Lizda Clark and Pennee Murphree dressed to 'Wow' at the Cotton Ball.

Whenever my family and I gather and recite our farm stories that occurred mainly in Maricopa, I often ask myself why so many of our relationships in Maricopa were and continue to be so rich? Why our bonds of friendship endure to this day? Then I answer my own question: We did life together. The best story to explain this involves my Mom and one of her best friends, Lizde Clark.

Every once in a while during any given week on the farm in Maricopa, Mom would dial Lizde's telephone number and a plan would emerge for that evening's meal.

"Hi, Lizde. I have a couple of pounds of hamburger, a few tomatoes, and some cheese to make tacos. Can you and Jay and the kids come over for supper, and we'll combine what we have?" In her distinctive Spanish accent, Lizda would say, "If you've got flour, I'll make the Tortillas, too, jes?"

"Oh wonderful," said Mom. "Sounds great. Come on over!"

At other times Lizde had the hamburger and Mom had the veggies. Fresh tortillas! They were our favorite. With flour flying, the Murphree kids, Brent, Patrick, Curt, and I, and the two Clark kids, John and Jacquie, tried to help with the tortilla making. We were mainly in the way. In the time it took the crowd of kids to make one, Lizde would make 10. And guess what, Lizde's tortillas were made with actual lard. The real stuff and they were the best!

Mom and Lizde's friendship was classic. Lizde and Jay, who lived about two miles down the road, had moved to Maricopa from Mexico to manage the Pecan Orchards for a company known as FICO (Farmers' Investment Company) about the same time Mom and Dad had moved there to farm. Lizde did not speak a word of English when they first met, and Mom spoke no Spanish.

But even an initial language barrier didn't keep Mom and Lizde from their invested adventures. One year Mom and Lizde decided to sew their own fancy dresses for the Annual Casa Grande Valley Cotton and Agriculture Women's Cotton Ball, the really "big deal" seasonal party held every December. During this same time, Mom and Lizde had been recruited to help in the pecan orchards Jay managed. So while Brent and I were off at school, Mom and Lizde set out to earn a little extra spending money picking pecans in the orchard. Between watching my two little brothers, Patrick and Curt, and John and Jacquie Clark, wiping runny noses, and sorting pecans,

Mom and Lizde forgot to put gloves on. When you pick pecans, an outer shell will terribly stain your hands if you don't wear gloves. Mom and Lizde went off to the Cotton Ball with their beautiful dresses completed but with black-stained hands.

Thinking back, it was as if life happened naturally and often spontaneously with family and good friends. Even if you had wanted to hide from your friends for a bit of seclusion, you couldn't. Everyone knew when you were home because though you might have a garage in which to park the cars, families never used the garage door. If you were home, you were visited.

Our relationships — who we hang out with — help define us. Broaden the circle of your friendships with quality people from all walks of life, and they'll enrich you. You'll do the same for them. ∞

MY PERSONAL JOURNAL

My Country Living Experiences

MY PERSONAL JOURNAL

My Country Living Experiences

_____

_____

_____

_____

_____

_____

_____

_____

_____

_____

_____

_____

_____

MY PERSONAL JOURNAL

My Country Living Experiences

_____

_____

_____

_____

_____

_____

_____

_____

_____

_____

_____

_____

_____

_____

MY PERSONAL JOURNAL

My Country Living Experiences

_____

_____

_____

_____

_____

_____

_____

_____

_____

_____

_____

_____

_____

_____

www.ingramcontent.com/pod-product-compliance
Lightning Source LLC
Chambersburg PA
CBHW030353290526
45785CB00004B/1725